Unbreakable Bonds

A Love that Lasts

Divina Nihalani

BookLeaf
Publishing

India | USA | UK

Dedication

To the dreamers, the lovers, the wanderers, and the quiet
souls who find beauty in the little things-
this book is for you.

May you always believe in the bonds that last forever.

Preface

Love is not just a fleeting emotion—it is the foundation
of who we are. It exists in the laughter of friends, in the
quiet strength of family, and in the gentle lessons of
time. It is unspoken yet deeply felt, fragile yet
unbreakable.

This collection, *Unbreakable Bonds – A Love That Lasts*,
is a tribute to the love that endures. Each poem captures
a different facet of the bonds we share, whether in
friendship, family, nature, or the quiet relationship we
hold with ourselves.

As you turn these pages, I hope you find reflections of
your own journey. May these words remind you that
love, in its truest form, is everlasting, unshaken by time,
distance, or change.

Thank you for allowing these poems to be part of your
world. May they echo in your heart long after you read
them.

Acknowledgements

A book is never created alone, and *Unbreakable Bonds – A Love That Lasts* would not exist without the love and support of so many.

To my family—your love is the foundation of all that I am. Thank you for being my constant source of strength and inspiration. My beloved partner who taught me what true love is.

To my friends—you are living proof of the bonds that stand the test of time. Your laughter, kindness, and unwavering support have shaped my words in ways I cannot express.

To the poets, writers, and dreamers before me—thank you for proving that love and art can outlive time itself. And most importantly, to you, the reader—thank you for picking up this book, for allowing these words to speak to you, and for carrying the love within these pages into your own life. May you always cherish the unbreakable bonds that make life beautiful.

Rooted in Love, Growing in Light

Born to a man so strong and true,
Who served the country with a steadfast view.
In a close-knit home where love ran deep,
With bonds so strong, they're ours to keep.

Danced through life with colors so bright,
Painting my dreams in laughter and light.
Married my love, my heart's true call,
Watched my brother make crowds enthrall.

Luxury lived, yet wisdom grew,
Found myself in all I do.
Saw my mother heal with grace so fine,
Her strength and care forever shine.

Through every turn, through highs and lows,
I walked my path as my soul chose.
Spreading joy in all I do,
With love, with art, with a heart so true.

Think Reverse- The Real Gift

We race ahead, we chase the prize,
But what if joy is in disguise?
Not in the rush, not in the race,
But in the smiles we learn to embrace!

Security's not just a lock and key,
It's laughter shared, it's feeling free.
Not piles of gold or walls so tall,
But knowing someone's there to call.

Think reverse—let's flip the view,
It's not just work, but fun times too!
A hug, a song, a carefree cheer,
The gift of love that stays so near.

So dance a little, take that chance,
Life's more than numbers in finance!
The safest place, the best delight,
Is love that holds us through the night.

Sassy, Wild & Bad Assy

She walks with fire, she talks with flair,
A rebel's heart, she owns the air.
Mystery wrapped in style so bold,
A story fierce, yet left untold.

She breathes in deep, exhales a dream,
Rules the world with self-esteem.
A little wild, a little sweet,
But never one to face defeat.

She laughs at limits, winks at fate,
Turns each fall into something great.
Swagger sharp, with heels so high,
She doesn't chase—she lets them try!

Bad assy moves, a queen so free,
Dancing through her destiny.
A force, a fire, a blazing light,
Too fierce to dim, too wild to fight!

Gravity of the Soul

Energy is magnetic, a force so true,
What you give, comes right back to you.
Be the person you'd long to stay near,
A soul full of warmth, no doubt, no fear.

Think through your heart, let logic play,
But love should lead, come what may.
Keep your books neat, but your spirit free,
Numbers align, but so should dreams.

Pack your bags, let's chase the sun,
Through winding roads and skies undone.
The Alps are calling, crisp and white,
A trek through peaks, pure delight.

Love so hard it shakes the ground,
A storm, a fire, a world unbound.
Let it mess you up, let it spin,
For love is chaos—but always wins.

Unleash the Fire

Greatness sleeps within your core,
A spark, a force, an open door.
Balance the chaos, steady your mind,
Focus sharp, leave doubt behind.

Start with purpose, finish strong,
Stamina builds as you move along.
Progress whispers, step by step,
Drive ignites where fear once slept.

Power rises, bold and bright,
Energize your soul, chase the light.
Vitality flows in those who dare,
Unleash the fire—breathe, prepare.

Right on Time, Just Like Wine

Tick-tock, chill—don't race the clock,
Life's got plans, so let it rock.
No need to chase, no need to beg,
What's meant for you is on its way!

Missed the train? Well, guess what, friend—
That wasn't your stop, not your end.
Every detour, every "no,"
Is just the world saying, "Not yet, though!

Good things age, just like fine wine,
Rushing won't make fate align.
So sip your coffee, dance, be free,
Trust the timing—wait and see!

One day soon, you'll laugh and say,
"Damn, it all worked out my way!"
So breathe, believe, enjoy the climb,
Your moment's coming—right on time!

Everything is Connected

Everything is connected, like a big, happy net,
Every smile and giggle is a treasure to get.
We switch our games, like colors in the sky,
Do what you love, let your dreams fly high.

I play with my toys and run in the park,
Every little moment lights a tiny spark.
I draw, I sing, and I dance with glee,
Because doing what I love makes me feel free.

Like puzzle pieces, all together we shine,
Each piece has a story, so special and fine.
When one fun game ends, a new one starts,
Just like a kite soaring high in our hearts.

Try a new song, give a new game a try,
Do what you love, reach for the sky.
Everything is connected, near and far,
Follow your dreams and be a shining star!

The word that sparked the day

In the hush of dawn, a word gleams bright,
A tiny spark igniting the morning light.
It whispers secrets only the brave can hear,
A playful riddle to make your spirit cheer.

The element of surprise dances in its sound,
A mystery waiting to be unbound.
Let it guide your steps, your curious heart,
Turning every moment into a work of art.

This word, a key to realms unknown,
Invites you to explore and truly own
The magic hidden in each surprise—
A carnival of wonder before your eyes.

So take this word, let it lead your way,
Transform the mundane into a bright ballet.
For every day holds a twist, a clue—
The unexpected magic that lives in you.

Melodies on the move

Cruising the city in a late-night cab,
Radio's playing—some old-school jazz.
The driver hums, the streets flash by,
Neon lights twinkle in the midnight sky.

A peppy tune, my fingers tap,
Lost in the music, no need for a map.
Focus fades, but who even cares?
Happiness hums in the evening air.

Traffic slows, but spirits stay high,
Positivity beams as headlights glide.
A caller jokes on the FM waves,
Laughter echoes—this night is saved.

Windows down, the breeze feels right,
Moments like these make hearts feel light.
No rush, no worries, just pure delight,
Cab rides and radio, a perfect night.

Radiant Heart Magic

In a garden of plenty, hearts overflow,
Every seed of kindness begins to grow.
The wealth of life isn't measured in gold,
But in love shared freely, warm and bold.

With a heart full of grace, I give with delight,
Spreading abundance like stars in the night.
Every gentle act, a luminous spark,
Igniting hope, banishing the dark.

Like a river that flows, never holding back,
My open heart follows its endless track.
For in each kind gesture, our spirits ignite,
We find our purpose, our inner light.

Abundance blooms in every caring deed,
In the art of giving, we truly succeed.
When hearts unite, the world feels anew—
A tapestry of love woven by me and you.

Happy Palette

With brush in hand and heart so free,
I splash the world with vivid artistry.
Each stroke's a giggle, every hue a grin,
A playful dance where joy begins.

I mix bright colors, bold and keen,
Creating dreams in every scene.
Happy content fills each space,
A burst of life in every trace.

I share my art with pure intent,
Spreading smiles wherever I went.
The world turns brighter, block by block,
As every line unlocks its shock.

A masterpiece born in light and cheer,
Fun and heartfelt, sincere and clear.
So join me now, let's play our part,
And paint our joy upon the heart.

Pages of Charm

In pages, magic awaits inside,
Words leap off the page, a joyful ride.
Reading whispers secrets of days long past,
Recalling memories that forever last.

Storytelling lights the night like a fire,
Filling hearts with dreams that inspire.
With every line, a new adventure starts,
Uniting voices, weaving art.

The power of reading opens minds wide,
Where memories and tales walk side by side.
Recalling each word, we revive our soul,
In the stories we share, we become whole.

Words bind us together, both near and far,
Lighting up life like a shining star.
So flip the page, let your spirit take flight,
For in every story, magic burns bright.

The Magic Minute

At 11:11, a magic moment gleams,
Whispering secrets in luminous beams.
Angel numbers chime, opening a hidden door,
Inviting bright ideas to soar and explore.

In that fleeting tick, creativity ignites,
Ideas shimmer like neon city lights.
Kindred souls glance up, smiles all around,
Finding wonder in the cosmic sound.

Events align in a playful, fated dance,
As the universe offers one more chance.
Laughter and dreams mix in the air,
A shared secret that all hearts can share.

At 11:11, time pauses to confide,
Revealing that magic lives on the inside.
A cosmic pulse that never fades away—
In that moment, hope and wonder hold sway.

Whispers of the Heart

Beneath everyday chatter, secrets quietly gleam,
Unsaid words shimmer like stars in a dream.
Hidden truths dance in the soft, silent air,
Whispering wisdom with playful flair.

Every heart cradles tales left unsaid,
Mysteries woven where spoken words dread.
Laughter and silence merge in a graceful art,
Revealing deep wonders that warm every heart.

In the pause of a smile, a secret unfurls,
Mystic reflections in a world full of pearls.
Unspoken feelings float like a gentle breeze,
Stirring hidden magic with effortless ease.

These playful echoes, wise and profound,
Spin life's mystery in each unvoiced sound.
In every quiet moment, a universe sings,
Unveiling deep truths on unspoken wings.

Soulventure

Not what they say, nor what they see,
But all you dream and wish to be.
A path unknown, yet still your own,
A voice once hushed, now loud and grown.

Through twists and turns, through loss and find,
You leave behind what's left confined.
For who you are is never set—
You are becoming, growing yet.

A step beyond the walls once built,
A freedom born beyond the guilt.
Not shaped by past, nor bound by fears,
But lessons learned through endless years.

The soul expands, the heart takes flight,
Through endless change, through seeking light.
For life's not meant to stay the same,
But bloom beyond what once had name.

Spirit of One

When morning breaks with a burst of fun,
The spirit of one shines bright like the sun.
It twirls through life with a quirky grin,
Turning every loss into a playful win.

Dancing on raindrops and skipping on dew,
It finds new adventures in all that's new.
Laughter guides the way like a trusty map,
Leaping over hurdles with a joyful clap.

This spirit is bold, with mischief and cheer,
Filling every moment with magic so clear.
It whispers of courage and dreams yet spun,
Painting life's canvas with colors undone.

A dash of mischief, a sprinkle of song,
It makes even dull days feel vibrant and strong.
So let your heart sing and let the fun run,
For the spirit of one brings magic to everyone.

Be You, Kiddo!

Kids, come along—let's have some fun,
Dance in the sun and laugh as one.
Every giggle is a burst of cheer,
Showing the world why you're so dear.

Play in puddles, spin under rain,
Let your wild spirit break every chain.
Build magic castles with every thought,
In your wondrous world, fun is always sought.

Embrace every quirk, every silly part,
For that's the art of your unique heart.
Sing off-key and dance out loud,
Stand tall and be marvelously proud.

Each day is a canvas—paint your own way,
Shine like a star, brighten your day.
Remember, kiddo, in all you do,
The best gift is simply being you.

Magic in the pause

In a cozy nook where time stands still,
A lazy hour unfolds by sheer will.
No tasks, no plans, just blissful repose,
Where quiet moments let the daydreams doze.

The mind unwinds in a gentle retreat,
Savoring nothingness, calm and sweet.
A cup of tea and soft, drifting tunes,
Dance with the clouds in lazy afternoons.

No pressure to hustle, no race to run,
Just soaking in moments beneath the sun.
Simple serenity fills the quiet air,
Proving that doing nothing is art beyond compare.

A gentle smile brightens the tranquil scene,
Revealing joy in spaces serene.
Embrace the pause, let worries depart,
For doing nothing is a gift to the heart.

Embrace It All

It's okay to smile, it's okay to cry,
To dance in the sun, or sigh at the sky.
Your heart may be heavy, or light as the breeze,
Emotions will come and go as they please.

Don't be too harsh, don't quiet your mind,
The gentlest thoughts are the easiest to find.
Let sadness speak, let joy arise,
Each feeling is wisdom in a new disguise.

Believe in the good, in kindness, in grace,
See love in the world, let it brighten your space.
An open heart, a soul set free,
Will always find peace in life's melody.

Zoom Out, Chill Out

Squint too close, and all you'll see,
Are tiny troubles bugging thee.
A little spill, a small delay,
Feels like the world is in dismay!

But take a step—or maybe ten,
Look again, now and then.
The puzzle's big, the view is wide,
Your worries shrink, so step aside!

That missed bus? A chance to roam.
That wrong turn? A way back home.
Life's a masterpiece, bold and grand,
Not just grains of scattered sand.

So zoom out, breathe, enjoy the ride,
The bigger picture is on your side!

Rewrite the Stars

Don't fear the blank page, don't hit rewind,
A fresh new chapter is yours to find.
The plot may twist, the script may flip,
But that's where all the magic drips!

Lost the map? Well, that's just fine,
X marks the spot—go redraw the line!
Erase, rewrite, scribble with flair,
Who said the rules were ever fair?

A story stuck is no good read,
So shake things up, plant a new seed.
Change the setting, swap the cast,
Make this version built to last!

Every restart is a thrilling cue,
A plot twist waiting just for you.
So start again—bold, unbothered, free,
This next edition? Pure mastery!

www.ingramcontent.com/pod-product-compliance
Lightning Source LLC
LaVergne TN
LVHW050507210726

843509LV00015BA/3029